In Winter Light

Tim Dooley is a tutor for The Poetry School and a mentor for the prison charity, Koestler Arts. He was reviews and features editor of *Poetry London* between 2008 and 2018, a visiting lecturer at the University of Westminster from 2016 to 2021 and a judge for the John Pollard International Poetry Competition at Trinity College Dublin in 2019 and 2020. He was previously a schoolteacher for many years. His poetry collections include *Discoveries* (Two Rivers Press, 2022) and the Poetry Book Society Recommendations: *Tenderness* (Smith Doorstop, 2003), *Keeping Time* (Salt, 2008), and *Weemoed* (Eyewear, 2017).

First published in the UK in 2022 by Two Rivers Press
7 Denmark Road, Reading RG1 5PA.
www.tworiverspress.com

Originals copyright © Éditions Gallimard 1977
Translations and Introduction copyright © Tim Dooley 2022

Permission to publish these translations has been granted
by Éditions Gallimard, Paris, France.

The right of Tim Dooley to be identified as the translator of the work
has been asserted by him in accordance with the Copyright, Designs
and Patents Act of 1988.

All rights reserved. No part of this publication may be reproduced,
stored in or introduced into a retrieval system, or transmitted,
in any form, or by any means (electronic, mechanical, photocopying,
recording or otherwise) without the prior written permission
of the publisher.

ISBN 978-1-909747-99-9

1 2 3 4 5 6 7 8 9

Two Rivers Press is represented in the UK by Inpress Ltd
and distributed by Ingram Publisher Services UK.

Cover design and illustration by Sally Castle
Text design by Nadja Guggi and typeset in Janson and Parisine

Printed and bound in Great Britain by Severn, Gloucester

In Winter Light

Philippe Jaccottet

translated by Tim Dooley

Poetry in translation by Two Rivers Press

Charles Baudelaire, *Paris Scenes* translated by Ian Brinton (2021)
René Noyau, *Earth on Fire and other Poems* translated by Gérard Noyau
  with Peter Pegnall (2021)
Maria Teresa Horta, *Point of Honour* translated by Lesley Saunders (2019)
Henri Michaux, *Storms under the Skin* translated by Jane Draycott (2017)
John Pilling & Peter Robinson (eds.), *The Rilke of Ruth Speirs:*
  New Poems, Duino Elegies, Sonnets to Orpheus & Others (2015)
Arthur Rimbaud, *The Drunken Boat* translated by Geoff Sawers (1999)

Also by Two Rivers Poets

David Attwooll, *The Sound Ladder* (2015)
William Bedford, *The Dancers of Colbek* (2020)
Kate Behrens, *Man with Bombe Alaska* (2016)
Kate Behrens, *Penumbra* (2019)
Kate Behrens, *Transitional Spaces* (2022)
Conor Carville, *English Martyrs* (2019)
David Cooke, *A Murmuration* (2015)
David Cooke, *Sicilian Elephants* (2021)
Tim Dooley, *Discoveries* (2022)
Jane Draycott & Lesley Saunders, *Christina the Astonishing*
  (re-issued 2022)
Jane Draycott, *Tideway* (re-issued 2022)
Claire Dyer, *Interference Effects* (2016)
Claire Dyer, *Yield* (2021)
John Froy, *Sandpaper & Seahorses* (2018)
James Harpur, *The Examined Life* (2021)
Ian House, *Just a Moment* (2020)
Rosie Jackson & Graham Burchell, *Two Girls and a Beehive* (2020)
Gill Learner, *Chill Factor* (2016)
Gill Learner, *Change* (2021)
Sue Leigh, *Chosen Hill* (2018)
Sue Leigh, *Her Orchards* (2021)
Becci Louise, *Octopus Medicine* (2017)
Mairi MacInnes, *Amazing Memories of Childhood, etc.* (2016)
Steven Matthews, *On Magnetism* (2017)

James Peake, *Reaction Time of Glass* (2019)
James Peake, *The Star in the Branches* (2022)
Peter Robinson & David Inshaw, *Bonjour Mr Inshaw* (2020)
Peter Robinson, *English Nettles* (re-issued 2022)
Lesley Saunders, *Nominy-Dominy* (2018)
Lesley Saunders, *This Thing of Blood & Love* (2022)
Jack Thacker, *Handling* (2018)
Robin Thomas, *The Weather on the Moon* (2022)
Susan Utting, *Half the Human Race* (2017)
Jean Watkins, *Precarious Lives* (2018)

Contents

'In the old days it would be called song' | viii

In Winter Light
   I. The Lessons | 1
   II. Songs from down there | 27
   III. In Winter Light | 47

'In the old days it would be called song'

The poems collected in *À la lumière d'hiver*, first published together in 1977, were written between 1966 and 1976 in Grignan, a small village in the Drôme area, to the north of Provence. Philippe Jaccottet (1925–2021) was Swiss by birth and, after studying in Lausanne, spent some years in Paris before deciding in 1953 to settle with his wife (the painter Anne-Marie Jaccottet) in the relatively isolated community where he spent the remainder of his life.

In Paris, Jaccottet had been encouraged by Francis Ponge, whose prose poems attended closely to the material world. Among his contemporaries, he became friendly with the poets Yves Bonnefoy and André Du Bouchet. He began finding work as a translator and his first collection of poems, *l'Effraie*, was published by Gallimard in 1953. Despite this success, he felt something of a provincial outsider. His move away from the city was prompted partly by economic necessity (he could live in Grignan on income from translation work, for which he was beginning to make a reputation, without having to resort to a teaching career) and partly because he felt he could function less self-consciously as a writer away from the company of more confident contemporaries.

In Grignan, Jaccottet immersed himself in his new surroundings. Regular walking in the countryside (something he'd done only rarely as a young man in Switzerland) became decisive for him as a writer. That observation of the natural world, the deeper knowledge of it he developed and the philosophical promptings it produced, bore fruit in his third collection of poems, *Airs* (1967), and in the first selection from the prose meditations of his notebooks, *La Semaison* (1971). The haiku-like poems in *Airs* catch particular moments seemingly isolated from the flow of time:

> At the stormy moment of daybreak
> at an exhausted moment in life
> these sickles in the close-cropped corn
>
> Cries suddenly so high up
> no hearing can reach them ('Swifts')[1]

Closeness to the natural world seems to have been less an escape or withdrawal for Jaccottet than a spur to a deeper exploration of consciousness. As he commented in an essay of this period, '...what I was writing, without my working at it particularly, became less and less unfaithful to the singularity of those profound experiences that moments of solitude and concentration bring to the surface.'[2]

The promise of a commission to translate the complete works of Goethe, which had been influential in Jaccottet's move to the country, could not be met by his publisher, but the poet instead began work on a translation of Homer's *Odyssey*. An exceptional work-rate over the next twenty years saw him translate, among others, Musil, Plato, Thomas Mann, Ingeborg Bachmann, and Giuseppe Ungaretti (with whom Jaccottet developed a close friendship). The most significant for his own work of the poets he translated, however, may have been Friedrich Hölderlin and Rainer Maria Rilke, both poets of exile and of the elemental.

Although Jaccottet, in marked contrast to many of his French contemporaries, has declared himself uninterested in formal philosophy, the interest in phenomenology and the philosophy of being that marked French intellectual life in the post-war years can still be traced in his writing. It may be worth reflecting that, in his essay 'What Are Poets For?', Martin Heidegger turned to Hölderlin and Rilke as forerunners who see the poet's role as 'to attend, singing, to the trace of the fugitive gods'.[3] The speaking subject in many of Jaccottet's poems shares such a sense of belatedness (he is 'betrayed by magic and the gods' in the opening section of 'À la lumière d'hiver'). This sense of solitude was linked in the thinking of the time with a determination to confront experience directly. Heidegger used a phrase from a manuscript poem of Rilke's to identify this acceptance of an unprotected state:

> in the end,
> It is our unshieldedness on which we depend,[4]

Jaccottet's speaker typically faces the world 'unshielded', without preconceptions. His task as a poet then becomes an attempt to arrive at a provisional order through attention to the world he finds himself in. In *La Semaison* he considers the possibility that such a sense of order might be a deception or a mirage:

> That mirage, or that intuition, revelation or dream, sets an order against disorder, a fullness against the void, and wonder, enthusiasm, hope against disgust. (...) And do we not have the

duty, or at least the right, to listen to that very deep, irresistible nostalgia within ourselves, as if it really said something important and true?[5]

The point is returned to in a film made for Swiss television in 1975[6] where Jaccottet recounts how, as a prisoner in one of Stalin's 'correction camps', the poet Osip Mandelstam hung on to a smuggled sonnet of Petrarch as a token of hope for himself and his fellow prisoners. To explain its power Jaccottet suggests that, in face of the worst, poetry can attest to a hidden or secret order that might act as a key and for an instant hold a prison door open. Without such an ambition, he adds, poetry would no longer be worth taking seriously.

In the poems that make up the three parts of *À la lumière d'hiver*, the need to assert 'wonder, enthusiasm, hope against disgust' faces a fiercer challenge than before. 'Leçons', the first of the three texts, was prompted by the death of Jaccottet's father-in-law, the printer Louis Haesler. Other deaths followed: Ungaretti in 1970, the poet Christiane Martin du Gard (a close friend) in 1973 and, after a serious illness, Jaccottet's mother in 1974.

The confrontation with mortality delineated in 'Leçons' includes both the observation of decline and the shock of absence, and follows the pattern of recognized stages of grief. Jaccottet has written explicitly about the difficulty involved in finding his way with the poem:

> The only one of my collections that caused real work, and took time, was *Leçons;* ... it didn't have the advantage, in its development, of the inner coherence that the previous books had had their origin in. I was split, and no careful work could repair that ruptured unity without the seams showing.[7]

In the opening sections of the sequence, Jaccottet castigates himself for thinking, in earlier poems (such as, perhaps, 'Le Livre Des Morts' in his second collection, *L'Ignorant*), that he 'could guide the dying and the dead'.[8] Instead he confronts the helplessness both of the suffering individual and of those who wish to comfort him:

> ... he seems a small child again,
> once more in a bed too big for him
> a child without the help of tears,
> with no help wherever he turns,

Two key terms used in 'Leçons', 'Maître' and 'mètre' are near homophones in French. Jaccottet uses the first to address the dying man, and sustains an extended metaphor of master and pupil through the sequence, while writer and reader study the lessons to be learned in the process of loss. 'Mètre' signifies both the metre of regular verse and the unit of measurement – and measure seems to be what is lost as we enter the world of the poem.

After a lightly rhymed prefatory quatrain, Jaccottet deploys free verse and often improvised punctuation to accompany his unsettling accounts. The poet's uncertainty is reflected in what he sees as science's incapacity to chart the passage from life to death. We are asked to consider where the person we have lost has gone to:

> If there is a place beyond distance,
> that ought to be where he is lost :
> neither further than any star, nor not as far,
> but already almost in another space,
> outside of it, dragged beyond measurement.
> Our metre rule can't reach from us to him;
> we'd be better snapping it across our knees.

If the metre rule is useless so too are the rules of metre, it seems, and with them the inner order that Jaccottet felt poetry should aspire to. The claims of religion are no better. Rather than a 'new birth' the final moments reveal 'no room between dry lips / for any bird to fly'.

The anger and denial give way to a calmer mood as funeral rites are considered and their consolations respected. In the final sections something like acceptance dawns as the poet pictures his view from a mountain, looking into and absorbing light. Here, he writes, 'for a second, embracing the circle of sky / around me, I think of death as something understood'. The 'master' resembles the sun and remains 'the model for our patient smiles'.

'Leçons' was published separately in 1969 and included in the selection *Poésie 1946–1967* published in 1971. It was changed substantially when it was incorporated into the 1977 volume along with 'Chants d'en bas' (also published on its own, in 1974, and changed slightly for the larger work). Jaccottet refers to both of these as 'livres de deuil' (books of mourning). 'Chants d'en bas', written during the months of his mother's final illness, is organised differently from

'Leçons', consisting of a poem in eight sections ('Parler'), preceded by an untitled elegy added in the 1977 edition, and followed by six 'Autres Chants'.

Where 'Leçons' was structured around a through narrative registering the often raw emotions prompted by loss, 'Chants d'en bas' acts as a series of interrogations, testing how poetry, and language itself, can respond to extremes of experience. The idea that poetry ('Speaking like this, / – in the old days it would be called song,') might be no more than 'a lie, an illusion' resurfaces from *La Semaison* – and in response comes a hesitant faith that the creative process might offer some redress:

> ...it's through open eyes
> these words are fed, as the trees
> are by their leaves.
> Everything we see
> and will have seen from childhood on,
> thrown down inside, mashed up, mis-shaped
> or soon forgotten (...)
> it all comes back as words,
> so lightened and purified that you think after
> you could even wade through death ... ('Speaking')

'Chants d'en bas' ends, as the previous sequence did, with an image of light as a healing power. Even when it 'drains away... and goes black', the writing hand insists on its existence by tracing its shadow with ink.

The dialogue with light dominates the final third of the book, which contains an introductory poem, 'Dis encore cela...', and the two-part title poem to both the volume and the section, 'À la lumière d'hiver'. The opening poem reiterates the hope that the 'weak, useless, unheard' voice of 'nameless victims' might be heard 'so that again / it might be possible to love the light'.

The first part of 'À la lumière d'hiver' considers how the poetic voice can be used to make suffering heard. Jaccottet makes light of his earlier preoccupations, playing on the title of a section of *Airs* called 'Oiseaux, Fleurs et Fruits' when he writes:

> Flowers, birds, fruit. It's true, I've made a home
> for them, watched them, put them on display, said :
> 'fragility is the true strength',
> easy to say!

To continue to write he has to be 'more / stubborn than that boy struggling, to carve his name / in the schoolroom desk'. Language can become a 'screen', hiding the 'still unknown' that it is the writer's duty to uncover.

The final part of the poem enters more visionary territory. A step into the garden on a winter night is crossing a threshold into the unknown. The night sky becomes an idealised feminine figure, the pursuit of her beauty a figure for the poet's quest. The migration of birds, the movement of farm animals at dusk, the germination of seed in the earth are all evidence of continuity of hope. It may not be possible to hold onto what is loved ('the whole world is an earthenware vase / in which I now see cracks are growing'), but the arrival of snow seems to offer a promise of transformation:

> Then I would remember this face
> which is also still there, behind
> the moist crystals' slow fall,
> shifting, clear-eyed, misty with tears,
> restless and faithful…
>   Behind the snow
> I would again pick out those clear blue eyes.

Although 'Leçons' and 'Chants d'en bas' had started life as separate volumes, the 1977 publication of *À la lumière d'hiver* by Gallimard made them part of a single work united by theme and language as much as by temporal proximity. It is recognised as marking an important stage in the poet's work: a bridge between the early lyric poems and the later work, which often integrates poems with prose meditations. Jaccottet continued to be prolific as a writer and his lifetime achievement was recognised when, in 2014, Philippe Jaccottet became the fifteenth living author and the fourth writer of Swiss birth to be published in the prestigious Bibliothèque de la Pléiade.

Parts of *À la lumière d'hiver* have appeared in English before. Cid Corman translated the 1971 text of 'Leçons' in *Breathings* (1974) and there was a recent version by Ian Brinton in *Long Poem Magazine 15* (2016). Derek Mahon included passages in his two collections of Jaccottet translations, *Selected Poems* (1988) and *Words in the Air* (1998), as did Jennie Feldman and Stephen Romer in their anthology *Into the Deep Street* (2009). This, however, is the first translation of the work as a whole.

I came across *À la lumière d'hiver* (on display in a bookshop in Quimper) in 1977, a few months after publication. At that time what excited me about Jaccottet's work was its linguistic scruple, the questioning of transparency that linked it in my mind with the poetry of WS Graham, whose *Implements in Their Places*, published in the same year, I had also been reading enthusiastically. I worked on English versions of some passages from the book over the years that followed. 'Speech', a version of 'Parler' from *Chants d'en bas*, appeared in my first collection of poems, *The Interrupted Dream* (Anvil, 1985) and 'Say That Again...' in an issue of the magazine *Perfect Bound*. Although I continued to read Jaccottet from time to time, it wasn't until 2015 that I returned to *À la lumière d'hiver* and, engaging now more fully with its theme of loss, began the version presented here.

In my first attempts I found myself adapting the syntax, punctuation and line division to my own practice, but the more I worked on the text the clearer it seemed to me that apparent idiosyncrasies in the poem's organisation were inseparable from its provisional way of working. I have therefore retained the run-on sentences and sometimes jagged line-breaks, which I take to be markers of uncertainty in the face of raw experience. I have benefited greatly from the advice of two poets with better linguistic knowledge than me, Hilary Davies and Terence Dooley. Each of them has guided me away from misreadings and imprecisions, and helped illuminate elusive passages. I am extremely grateful for their help. Any remaining misunderstandings are my own responsibility.

Tim Dooley

Notes

1 Jaccottet, Phillipe, 'Martinets', *Airs*, Gallimard, 1967, p. 33, my translation.

2 Jaccottet, Phillipe, '"Cette folie de se livrer nuit et jour à une oeuvre..."', *La Nouvelle Revue Française*, March 1976. Collected in *Une Transaction Secrète*, Gallimard, 1987, p. 320, my translation.

3 Heidegger, Martin, 'What are Poets For?', *Poetry Language Thought* translated by Albert Hofstader, Harper, 1971, p. 92.

4 ibid p. 97.

5 Jaccottet, Phillipe, *Seedtime (La Semaison)* translated by André Lefèvre, *New Directions*, 1977, p. 7.

6 https://www.youtube.com/watch?v=uOog79nH8qs 'Philippe Jaccottet en personne', DOCUMENTAIRE, 1975. Accessed 22 March 2019.

7 Jaccottet, Phillipe, '"Cette folie de se livrer nuit et jour à une oeuvre..."', *La Nouvelle Revue Française*, March 1976. Collected in *Une Transaction Secrète*, Gallimard, 1987, p. 321, my translation.

8 The self-referential play on words begins in the second line of this section where the speaker describes himself as 'l'effrayé, l'ignorant' ('fearful, ignorant'), bringing to mind the titles of Jaccottet's earlier collections *l'Effraie* ('The Screech-Owl') and *l'Ignorant*.

I. The Lessons

*Let him stand in the corner. Let him measure,
as he once set type, the lines that I assemble,
questioning, recalling his end. Let his sure
gaze keep my hand steady, should it tremble.*

Once,
fearful, ignorant, barely living,
and blindfolding myself with images,
I presumed I could guide the dying and dead.

Sheltered, a poet
spared pain, barely knowing it existed,
I thought I'd chart the way to that end!

Now, the lamp blown out,
my trembling hand wavers,
starting again, slowly tracing paths in the air.

Fig-trees and vines
ripening far away in the mountains
under slow-moving clouds
and the cooling wind :
of course, of course…

A moment comes when the old man lies down
with almost no strength left. You notice
from day to day how
his steps are less certain.

It's not the movement
of a stream through the grass :
something's not right.

Now my very own teacher
has been taken so far away so fast,
I can't think what will come after him :

not the lantern-fruit,
not the far-flying bird,
not the purest image;

rather fresh water and linen,
the protecting hand,
the heart that endures.

The only thing I want to do
is shift whatever blocks the light from us,
only leaving some room
for disregarded kindnesses.

I listen to old men
who have come to terms with their days,
I sit at their feet to learn patience :

I'm their worst student by far.

If not the first thunderclap it's the first lightning-flash
of sorrow : that our master, our seeding plant
should be thrown so low
that the good teacher should be punished
so that he seems a small child again,
once more in a bed too big for him,
a child without the help of tears,
with no help wherever he turns,
cornered, pinned down, drained.

He hardly weighs a thing.

The ground we stood on trembles.

A dazed look
began to be seen in his eyes : could that
be possible. A sadness too
as huge as what was coming towards him,
knocking down the green and bird-filled
boundaries of his life.

He who had always loved his walled, secluded garden,
who kept the keys of the house.

Though the distance between us
and the furthest star is unimaginable,
it's still a line, a link, a pathway of sorts.
If there is a place beyond distance,
that ought to be where he is lost :
neither further than any star, nor not as far,
but already almost in another space,
outside of it, dragged beyond measurement.
Our metre rule can't reach from us to him;
we'd be better snapping it across our knees.

(Measure, you hard-tasked brains, yes, measure
what separates us from yet unknown stars,
plot the path, as if blind drunk, follow the lines,
then look at the broken ruler in your hands.
Now consider the only space you can't enter.)

Silent. The bond of words begins to unravel
as well. He slips words out.
Frontier. For a little while
we can still see him.
He can hardly hear any more.
Should we try to get this stranger's attention if he's forgotten
our tongue, if he no longer stops to listen?
He has business elsewhere.
He no longer has business with anything.
Even when he's turned to face us,
it's as though we could only see his back.

That back so stooped,
what's he trying to crawl under?

'Who will help me? No one can reach me here.
Whoever holds my hand steady can't steady the shaking,
who screens my eyes can't stop me seeing, those
who surround me night and day like an overcoat
can't keep me from this heat, this cold.
From here, I can promise you there is a wall
no battering ram or trumpet will bring down.
From now on all that's left is the long worst thing.'

Is this what he doesn't say in the narrow passage of night?

It's above us now
like the overhang on a mountain.

Under its icy shadow
you can either stand in awe or throw up.

You hardly bear to look.

Something gives way to ruin.
How sad it is
when the other world wedges itself
into the body.

Don't expect me
to bring light and steel together.

On this cold day
face against the mountain's wall
we are filled with pity and horror.

On a day bristling with birds.

Call it horror, call it filth,
use the filthiest words you can find,
read out your dirty linen :
whatever monkey business poets succumb to,
it doesn't get onto the writer's page.

Filth you can't speak of, can't look at,
but have to swallow.

And yet it's
as simple as dirt.

Couldn't even the thickest night
cover this with a blanket?

Infinity couples or tears apart.

You catch the stale smell of old gods.

Bereft
as if a mountain collapsed on us.

It takes something more than the passing of a dream
to tear you apart in this way.

If a man were only a knot of air,
should it need such sharp steel to cut him open.

Each of us a bundle of tears, face to the wall,
what this is teaching us
isn't the mutability of one man's life
but the reality of ours.

It's being whipped into us.

A simple breath, a light knot of air
a seed escaped from Time's wild grass,
just a voice flying in song
across shadow and light,

they fade : no trace of injury.
Better to say that the voice, in an instant,
wipes out the peaceful plain, the purer day.
Who are we that we must have iron in the blood?

He is torn out, scratched,
the room we held each other in is torn apart,
each fibre of our being cries out.

What if 'the veil of Time' were torn
or 'the body's cage' split open
or this were a 'new birth'?

Then we could pass through the eye of the wound,
we could enter the eternal, alive…

You calm, serious midwives,
have you heard the cry
of a new birth?

All I've seen is the wax left when the flame is out,
and no room between dry lips
for a single bird to fly.

Not a single breath.

Like when the morning wind
got the better
of the last candle.

Ours is such a deep silence
we could catch
the sound of a comet streaming through the night
to our daughter's daughters.

Already it's no longer him.
Breath snatched-out : unrecognizable.

A corpse. A comet is closer to us.

Take that away.

A human being – this accident of the air,
something closer to hail in a thunderstorm than an insect
                                         of netting and glass;
this rock of smiles and simmering good will;
this vase made heavier by deeds, by memories –,
snatch the breath from it : it rots.

Who seeks revenge, for what, with such a lump of spit?

We ought to clean the place.

I looked up.

Outside the window,
in the depths of the day,
images still drift by.

Shuttles, or angels of being,
weaving over the gap.

The child chooses a toy, an earthenware boat,
to lay near the dead man;
will the Nile flow on into this heart?

I used to notice those boat-shaped tombs
made in the shape of the horned moon.
I don't think the soul needs a boat these days,
nor scented oils, nor card of passage to the underworld.

What if a child's gentle fancy
could leave our world, could
reach what nothing else could reach?

Or is it meant to console us, left on the shore?

If it could ever be possible these days
(and who will ever know?) to believe
some being, some consciousness maybe,
might remain at hand, would he choose this place –
the walled garden, not the open meadow?
Could he then have waited here,
as if we'd arranged to meet 'just by the stone',
and made use of our muffled steps, our tears?
Who knows? One day or another, these stones
will sink beneath the perennial grass,
sooner or later there'll be no visitors
to the marking stone, buried in its turn,
and no more shades where there is no shade.

Rather, now the business is over, I've had only one wish:
to rest my back against the wall
not to look away from daylight any more,
but to help the waters that rise in these mountains

dig out a cradle in the grass
and bring me, across the August nights,
under the low branches of the fig trees,
barges loaded with the warmth of sighs.

Now I'm completely inside the sky's cascade,
wreathed in a mane of air,
hanging here just below the buzzards,
on a level with the light-filled leaves,
looking
listening
– and the butterflies are so many dying flames,
the mountains so much smoke –,
for a second, embracing the circle of sky
around me, I think of death as something understood.

I can hardly see anything other than light,
the distant bird-calls are knots of light,

the mountain?

A light falling of ash
at the foot of day.

You on the other hand

either completely wiped away
leaving us fewer ashes
than an evening's fire in the hearth,

or invisible inhabiting the invisible,

or a seed lodged in our hearts,

whichever it is

you're still the model for our patient smiles,
like the sun warming our backs, bringing light
to the table, and the page, and the grapes.

II. Songs from down there

I've seen her upright and trimmed with lace
like a Spanish candle.
Now like her own candle, she has gone out.

She seems suddenly hard to me!

Hard as a stone,
a chip of stone knocked into the light,
an axe cutting through the bole of the air.
And these unseeing birds
still fly across the garden, still sing
in the light in spite of it all!

Now she is her own stone,
a few well-meant, pointless flowers on top
and no name : stone too-little loved,
deep in the sapwood of the heart.

Speaking

I

Speaking is easy, and in putting words on paper
you don't take too many chances as a rule;
it's work for a lace-maker, something cosy
and placid (we might have asked for
the candle's softer, more beguiling light)
all the words are written in the same ink,
'angel' and 'anger' for example are almost the same,
and I could easily write 'blood' on every line
of it, the page would stay unstained,
and I would not be hurt.

Then sometimes it comes to seem a horrible game,
now you can't understand what you were playing at,
when you might have taken your chances outside
and done something useful with your hands.

That
is when you can no longer steal away from grief,
which is like a figure approaching,
tearing at the mist that's around you,
knocking down obstacles one by one, crossing
the ever-shrinking distance – suddenly so near
all you see is a huge snout
blocking the sky.

Then speaking seems a pretence, or something worse :
a coward's snub to grief, a squandering
of the little time and strength that we have left.

2

Everyone has seen once (though these days
they try to keep us even from the sight of fire)
what happens to a sheet of paper near a flame,
how it curls up, at the last minute, shrivels,
unravels itself, frayed... That can happen to us, as well,
this convulsive withdrawal, always too late
and always starting again; it goes on for days,
always more feeble, frightened, abrupt,
facing what is worse than fire.

Though it destroys, fire still has a glory,
at least it's red, you could call it a tiger,
a rose, at a push you could pretend,
and picture yourself desiring it
like a body, or a form of speech,
put another way, it's the eternal theme
of a poem, it kindles the page
and suddenly with a stronger livelier flame
lights up the room all the way to the bed or the garden
and doesn't burn you – on the contrary,
it's as though you were the heart of the fire
as if it gave you breath and you were
a young man again looking out on
a future without end...

It's something else, much worse, that makes a person
shrivel up inside himself, draw back to
the room's far wall, calling
for anyone to help, calling for anything :
this has no shape, nor face, nor any name;
you can't make it tame with delightful images
or obedient with grammar,
it tears the page the way
it tears skin,
it stops us speaking except in animal sounds.

3

Yet speaking is something more, or can be,
than shielding oneself with air or straw....
It can be like April, the first warm days
when each tree becomes a spring, when night
seems to stream with the voices of a cave
(you'd think we'd have something better to do
in the fresh-leaved dark, than sleep),
it rises in you like a sort of happiness,
as if you had no choice, as if you needed to release
some pent-up energy, to give back freely to the wind
the drunkenness you sipped from the fragile wine glass of dawn.

Speaking like this,
– in the old days it would be called song,
and now we hardly dare do it –
is it a lie, an illusion? Yet it's through open eyes
these words are fed, as the trees
are by their leaves.
                              Everything we see
and will have seen from childhood on,
thrown down inside, mashed up, mis-shaped
or soon forgotten – *the boy's procession*
from school to graveyard through the rain;
an ancient lady in black, sitting at
the high window from where she gazes into
the saddler's shop; a yellow dog called Pyramus
in the garden where an espaliered wall
brings back the echo of a shooting party,
fragments, wreckage of years –

it all comes back as words,
so lightened and purified that you think after
you could even wade through death .....

4

Could there be things that live in words
easily, harmoniously
– moments of happiness recaptured in poems
with happiness, a light transcending words,
almost obliterating them – and other things
which kick against them, warp and break them :

as if words rejected death,
or, rather, death rotted
even words?

5

Enough! enough.
Destroy the hand that can only
write in smoke,
and look with open eyes :

The boat of bones that carried you sails off,
it founders (and the deepest thoughts
won't heal its joints),
it fills with bitter water.

If there is no great net of light
we dare hope for,
accord at least to old human vessels
on death's shores, remission of sentence,
softer breezes, childhood sleep.

6

I would like to have spoken without images, simply
pushing open the door...
                              I'm too fearful,
impatient, compassionate even, for that :
we can't live like birds, out a long time
in the open, blatant sky,
                                    as we fall back to earth
all we see clearly of them are images
or dreams.

7

Speaking is difficult then, if it's a quest... what's it seeking?
A fidelity to the only moments, only things
that go deep enough inside us, that evade us,
or is it plaiting a loose shelter for an untrappable prey...

What if it's wearing a mask more real than your face
to celebrate a long-forgotten festival
with others dead, distant, still asleep,
and this whisper, these stumbling first steps, these shy flames
– our words –
scarcely rise from their slumber :
rustling of a drum should the unknown finger
brush its skin...

8

Rip up this darkness finally to rags,
patchwork penitent, phony beggar, shroud-chaser;
it's shameful to ape death from afar,
it'll be enough to be afraid when it's time. For now
wrap yourself up in the sun's furs, go out
like a hunter into the wind, push through
your life as if crossing cold rapids.

If you could be less afraid,
you might not cast a shadow on your tracks.

*(I could tear your tongue out, sometimes,
sententious phrase-maker. Look at you now
in front of the mirror the witches hold for you.
Golden mouth, proud source of sonorous prodigies,
you're nothing more a dribbling sewer.)*

Other songs

What have we made of our lives, old friends,
our blood is thinner, our hopes cut short,
we've become cautious and stingy and short of
breath – old guard dogs with nothing very much
to guard or bite –
we've started to look like our fathers....

Is there no chance of conquering this
or at least of avoiding defeat before our time?
We heard the sombre hinges of age creaking
that day we first caught ourselves
walking head turned back to the past,
ready to take on the crown of our memories...

Is there no other way
than trailing off with rambling pearls of wisdom,
labyrinthine lies and poor foolish fear?

Something different from the imposture
of the ageing beau's rouge and perfume,
or the groaning of the blunted instrument,
or the stammering of the madman to his
aggressive, insomniac, faceless companions?

If we can no longer deal with the visible
world, if beauty is really no longer for us
– lips trembling as the dress is unbuttoned –,
let's look more deeply still,
let's look further, where words slip away,
and we don't know what leads us, what blind
shade, or patient, shade-coloured hound.

If there's a passage out of here, it isn't visible,
if there's a lamp to guide us, it isn't one that
a maid might carry two steps ahead of the guest
– and one hand would blush shielding the flame,
as she opened the door with her other –
if there were a password, it wouldn't be enough to
set it down here like a clause in an insurance policy.

Let's search for something beyond our grasp, with some stretch,
or leap in the dark, or mindless chance that the words
'seek' or 'find' can't capture....

Friends starting to grow old and distant.
I try to avoid going over the same tracks
– *remember the rowan, remember the hawthorn
burning for the Easter Vigil...* and the heart
softening then, blubbing over the ashes –
I try,

but there's almost too much
to carry on the dark path I see us going down,
and who can put things right with the unseen
each day? who ever could?

Whether in dreams or not, but always penned in
by the haze of night – we'll have seen such women :
under their mare's manes flashes of fire
and long tender eyes shining like leather,
not the flesh offered on these new linen stalls,
cheap, everyday, ready to be guzzled between two sheets
but the sister creature, who shies away and shows herself,
hardly more distinct from her curls and lace
than the sea's motion is from its spray and spume,
lithe creature that all are tracking,
that the best equipped hunter will never catch
since she is hidden deeper within her body than
he can ever reach – though he roars with an assumed victory,
since she is only the gateway
to her own garden,
or a fault that appears in the night
but leaves the wall unshaken, a trap
streaming with the scent of fruit, a fruit
that will earn a glance – and tears.

If I lay my head against the earth,
will I hear her tears down below,
footsteps dragging along icy corridors or
stumbling as they flee through abandoned districts?

In my head I can see night-time streets,
more misremembered rooms and faces
than the leaves of summer trees and each
of them filled with thoughts and images
– like some maze in a hall of mirrors
that's badly lit with dingy lanterns –
when we were young at the fairground
I thought I knew the way out,
I used to yearn for certain bodies.
I've a head filled with tricks of light, with
reflections, inlets to a river of shadow,
I remember the gaping mouths along its banks –

that's all I'm hearing now from under the ground
as I lie with my head on the grass,
above the thunder of her fear and the
sawing sounds of the insects' moans –
call it what you like, she's there for certain.
she's down there, in the dark, and she's crying.

Wait, child : this is not for your eyes,
close them a moment, blinded in sleep,
stay ignorant a moment longer, so your eyes
resemble the innocent sky.

Take in the birds and the light
one more time,
you are growing into a glittering aspen,

or take a step back – before this harpoon
leaves you shrieking with fear

Write this book quickly, finish this poem quickly,
today, before self-doubt catches you out once more :
that storm of questions that misleads you and leaves
you stumbling or worse...
                                  Run to the end of the line,
fill up the page before your hands begin to tremble
with fear – of being misled, of illness, of showing fear –
before the air gives up the beautiful blue wall
you hope to lean against a little longer.
Already the great clock misses a beat sometimes in its belfry of bone
and staggers as if cracking the walls.

Don't dedicate this 'To the Angel of the Laodicean Church'
but write without knowing who you write for, write
in the air with the anxious, hesitant movements of a bat,
quick, fill this space up again with your hand,
bind it up, sew it together hastily, but clothe us,
we are animals who feel the cold, awkward moles,
cover us with a last golden panel of light
just as the sun does the poplars, the mountains.

I steady myself with difficulty and look out :
let us say there are three lights.
The light of the heavens, the light that comes from beyond
but drains away in me and goes black,
the light whose shadow on the page I'm tracing with my hand.

The ink could be made of shadow.

I'm surprised that the sky moves above me.

People like to believe that we're made to suffer
for a clearer sight of heaven. But suffering
puts all that to flight, and pity
drowns it, shining with as many brilliant tears
as the night sky.

III. In Winter Light

Say that again…

Say that again, patiently, more patiently
or furiously, but say it again
despite the tormentors, try to say it
despite the strap-strokes of time.
                          Hope that the fugitive's last cry,
at the point of collapse, will be like this,
weak, useless, unheard,
so he might save himself, if not his skin,
from the bullet's unswerving trajectory
and his cry might be picked up by some other ear than
the great open earth, somewhere above, no not above,
elsewhere, not elsewhere, could be received
perhaps below, in the way water
sinks into the garden's dry earth,
the way blood is spilt at random
in the unknown.

Last chance for all nameless victims :
that there may be, not beyond hills
or clouds, nor above the sky,
nor hidden behind bright eyes and
beautiful breasts, but somehow,
mixed in with the world we pass through,
that there might be, animating the smallest particles,
something the voice cannot name, something
nothing can measure, so that again
it might be possible to love the light
or solely take it in
or simply see it still
see her, as the earth receives her,
and not just a trace of ash.

In winter light

I

Flowers, birds, fruit. It's true, I've made a home
for them, watched them, put them on display, said :
'fragility is the true strength',
easy to say! and so easy to juggle
with weighty things once you've wrapped them in words!
We built Elijah's chariot of fire from light seeds,
whispers and sparks – we made out we were
clothed in air like birds or blessed saints…

Indistinct signs, a house of mist and gleams,
youth…
          then creaking doors close on you
one by one.

All the same I still use words,
not lifted up by the rush of blood or wings,
no longer spellbound,
betrayed by magic and the gods,
abandoned long ago by the nymphs
who languished by the banks of clear streams
or lay in the light of dawn,
                      but trying to speak, I'm more
stubborn than that boy struggling to carve his name
in the schoolroom desk,

I keep at it whether I know the words any more,
whether or not this is the right path
– which is straight as the flight of love
to the target, the rose, the evening sun,
but I only have a dim cane
which can't even pick out a path, but wrecks
the last grasses growing in the verges, sown
I'd guess in daylight, for someone
more sure-footed than me…

'Well, it's true, I've seen death at work,
and, as well as death, the effects of time
close to me, on me, I confirm it with both eyes.
Settled! There's scarcely time to list our aches and pains.
But something remains unharmed by this knife, or else
repairs itself after a cut, as water reassembles behind a boat.'

'Throw time's stones at me again, stones
that destroyed the fairies and the gods,
so I may learn to cope with their flight and fall.'

If it were something between other things, like the space
between the linden and the laurel, in the garden,
like the cold air that greets the mouth and eyes
when, not stopping to think, you cut through your life,
yes, if it was such a simple careless step
outside…
               A delicate thought, but how can thought
patch the body together, if the stuff of it is tearing apart?

An ageing man is packed tight with rigid
images lined like iron through his life
– don't expect him to sing with nails in his throat.
Once light lived in his voice,
now he speaks for reason and restraint.

Well we can talk coolly about sadness and joy,
you'd think it almost too easy to demonstrate
the pointlessness of life. Anyone
can speak as I do now, in this room
which is still intact, through lips
which haven't finally been sealed with
the thread of death.
                                  Anyway, it's fair to say that
this sort of discourse – to the point or wasteful of words,
but either way authoritarian and blindly obscure –
won't hit the mark any more, won't hit home at all,
turning around on itself endlessly, utterly empty,
while, somewhere further away or perhaps just
to one side, the thing your words searched for so long
was waiting. Should words then make us feel
the thing they can't reach, what escapes them,
the underside they'll never master?

Once again I've lost myself in them,
once again they've put up a screen. I can't find
the correct expression,
                              while ever further away
the golden key, the still unknown reveals itself
and the light already fading, the light of my eyes...

II

Cold, black, ice-black, crystalline air help me
now. The weightless leaves shift almost
subliminally, like the thoughts of a sleeping child.
Crossing this empty space, it's as if time stepped
across the garden, stepping above us between
slates and stars, night itself walking by.

I take these few steps before starting back,
to where I no longer know what's waiting for me,
a tender lover or one who's turned away,
a dream of attentive servants
or the same imploring face...
the fading light of day
                              – as if a veil had fallen
leaving these pretty, naked feet
visible for a second –
                           reveals the crystal ebony
beauty, the black silk woman
whose glances still shine at me from lights
snuffed out maybe centuries ago.

Daylight is in retreat, revealing
as time passes and I follow in its steps
across the garden
                     something else
– beyond the relentless pursuit of that beauty,
that belle of the ball to which no-one was invited,
those gold clasps on a dress quite lost to fashion,
something more deeply hidden, yet closer...

The shadows are muted. Bushes tremble. Even colours
begin to close their eyes as darkness washes over
the earth.
                It's as if day's great
painted door swung on its invisible hinges.
I go out in the night. I go out at last.
I cross over and, in my steps,
time too crosses the threshold.
                                Blackness is no longer
the soot-stained wall smeared by the work of day,
I break through it to the clear and silent air,
I go forward at last among the still leaves,
at last, I can make a few tentative steps,
light as the air's own shadow,

time's wing shines and runs through the black silk,
but I no longer hold on to a measuring rule,
there's only freshness, an unfamiliar freshness,
whose scent comes back to me just before dawn.

(Such a small thing, just a few steps outdoors,
yet more uncanny than the magi or the gods.)

A stranger has slid in among my words,
wearing a beautiful lace mask meshed with
two pearls, various pearls, tears or looks.
She's no doubt escaped from the world of dreams,
brushing past me in her dress as she goes on her way.
– or was that black silk really her skin, or her hair? –
and already I'm chasing after her, weak
and getting older, as if trying to recover a memory;
but I won't catch up with her any more than the others
I waited for at the school gates or the porter's lodge,
doors closed to me by swiftly passing days...

I don't think I should have let her into
my heart; but can't I make a little space
for her, where she could come close?
– I don't know her name but I've drunk her perfume,
her breath, the murmur were she to speak –
forever unapproached, she begins to fade
and pass just as the paper lanterns light up
on the acacia trees.

Allow me to let her pass, having seen her once again,
then I'll leave without her having noticed.
I'll climb up a few tired steps,
relight the lamp and take up the page again
with simpler words and truer, if I can.

November clouds, shadow-striped birds,
you trail through the mountains
leaving a few breast-feathers behind you,
the long mirrors of deserted roads, ditches,
the earth harder than ever to ignore,
grave and cradle of what grows;
                                        will we soon
no longer grasp the secret you're bound up in?

Listen, listen carefully, behind all
the walls, across the growing uproar
that's as much inside you as outside,
listen… And take from that hidden water
where, it seems, those unseen figures still drink
in the steps of those creatures, silent, pale and slow
who've been coming forever at sunset
(in honour of the sun that's shone on the meadow since dawn),
to drink deeply from this light that doesn't go out night
but is just barely covered in shadow,
as the flocks cloak themselves with a blanket of sleep.

… And will the sky be so mild all winter
when the farmhand has ploughed the earth with patience
or maybe Venus will have peeked out once or twice
between the mud and the mist of dawn,
will the razed earth bring forth in March
any other growth than grass?

Everything that comes back to me – often very little –
is it just a dream or from a dream
is there some echo we should hang onto
as if protecting an essential flame from extinction by the wind
or should it be poured out as a libation
on the soil we cross with stumbling, slow steps
before we sink into it? (It's collapsing already.)

The water that we'll never drink, the light
these weak eyes won't glimpse,
I've still not lost the thought of them…

But dawn's wine-glass is quickly broken,
the whole world is an earthenware vase
in which I now see the cracks are growing,
and this skull is a flask made of bone
soon ready for disposal.

What does it hold anyway but water
which can be bitter or sweet to drink?

Tears sometimes rise to the eyes
as if from a spring,
they are like the mist rising on the lakes,
a clouding of inner light,
a water turned salty with sadness.

Perhaps all we can ask of those distant gods,
of the deaf, blind gods who turned their backs on us,
of those deserters,
might be that each tear shed
on a face close to us
should cause to germinate
an unfailing crop in the unseen land.

Winter, evening :
                      sometimes, this space
seems like a panelled room,
its blue curtains gradually darkening
as the last glimmers of fire waste away;
then the snow brightens the wall
as if a lamp of cold light.

Or is it the moon rising already,
washing the dust from us
and the moist breath from our mouths?

Listen, see : isn't something rising out of
the earth, from somewhere far below,
something like a light, coming in waves, like a wounded
Lazarus, surprised, coming in the slow beating of white
wings – just as everything becomes hushed,
here, truly, where we stand afeared –,
and isn't it coming to us from beyond the sky,
meeting other, brighter, flying things
– untrammelled by muddy origins –
and aren't they now running towards one another
faster and faster like lovers rushing
to their embrace?

Yes, think it, whatever it might be, say it,
say it's possible to see such a thing,
that you still know how to run like that,
though you're wrapped round by the rough blanket of night.

What I'd like to see now,
is snow falling slowly,
settling through the day on the world of things
– murmuring as ever with her low voice –
so that the seeds sleep more patiently
with such protection.

And we would know all the time the sun
was still there; so if the snow tired,
the sun would let himself be seen again
like a candle behind a yellowing screen.

Then I would remember this face
which is also still there, behind
the moist crystals' slow fall,
shifting, clear-eyed, misty with tears,
restless and faithful…
                                   Behind the snow
I would again pick out those clear blue eyes.

Faithful eyes weakening until
mine close, and after them the firmament,
like a painted fan frayed to its bare bone
handle, an icy trail of the only
unblinking eyes among the stars.

Two Rivers Press has been publishing in and about Reading
since 1994. Founded by the artist Peter Hay (1951–2003),
the press continues to delight readers, local and further afield,
with its varied list of individually designed,
thought-provoking books.

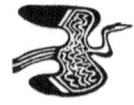